# Les Petits Mots

en noir

Disha

Made with ❤ on the BookLeaf Publishing Platform

www.bookleafpub.in

www.bookleafpub.com

# Dedication

*To the hands that brought me to life*
*not the first but the second time.*

# Preface

Each poem in this collection is a doorway to an emotion, a moment, a fragment of life captured in verse. These words are whispers of joy, echoes of sorrow, and reflections of the unspoken. May you find yourself in these pages, in the spaces between the lines, and in the emotions they awaken.

# Acknowledgements

To everyone who held space for my words,
and to those who made me feel deeply enough to write
them.
Thank you, truly.

# 1. You to me, Me to you

You were a name, a voice, a screen,
Yet more than all I'd ever seen.
I held my storms, you held your scars,
Together we made a home under the stars.

For every heart that beats as one,
This deal follows through till all is done
For you to me
And me to you
Will always be like tides and moons.

One seeks refuge, the other grace,
One finds a home, the other space.
At any point of time
Without a thought, without a why
They know how to hold
They know to try .

Bounded in a bond or a knot or a crime
The ties we weave in comes in different forms and style
With friends, with blood, with fleeting norms and tribes
You learned that I needed you in my life.

Not just to love or to feel pride
But to read the signs, to stand with time.
One gives, one takes, one aches, one thrives,
Not all weights are equal; yet love survives.

# 2. Desire

A traveler never sleeps;
He dreams about places.
A home he never got,
His desires mistreated.
A pink that starts fading,
His lips laced with secrets,
Turning red whenever he lies.
I wish he were all mine.

# 3. The Room That Speaks

My heart is the one
That tells me to listen to none.
They see my face,
They see my hands,
Yet they fail to read my lips
And the words my lines chant.

You come into my room,
You see a box of grief,
A couple, I believe.
A mirror that tells you the truth,
Probably a frame or two that lie so smooth.

But once you lock the door,
You'll feel the pillow as stone as the floor.
The walls will talk about their day.
They'll ask you if you are here to play.
And the little girl sitting in the corner
Prays that you stay.

# 4. A reason to everything

There is a reason to everything,
And a lie for all beings.
The words that I fell for
Were the ones you once stood for.

I have been driving in the dark,
Still feel you living along the park.
The same land we used to share,
For each other we used to care.

No stress, no cry,
No tears becoming dry.
Those hours aren't mine anymore;
The ones I own broke me more.

The soul is yours, yet it feels mine,
Then there is mine, working 8 to 9,
Coming back home bruised,
Hoping to be rescued.

At last, there is a sigh.
She saw a phoenix up high.
There rose a hope,
And she was saved by a pixie rope.

# 5. Seeds Beneath the Floorboards

This prison of my own I keep finding a way out
Might not be the result of my doing.
I feel the floor shiver perhaps on purpose,
So I could hide the seeds I have been sowing,

In the small patch of land, or was it a pot filled with soil,
Given to me as a sign of hope.
To water it, to watch it grow,
Counting days to track its growth
Was perhaps my way to cope.

With all the rules, all the fights,
All the people leaving at the first sight of our lives.
They think we don't speak, they think we don't eat.
Little do they know how full we already feel.

A masquerade ball is what every party seems to us;
The masks we wear conceal our fear.
Isn't that a small price to pay for our safety?
To whom does it matter that we live with sanctity?

# 6. Love at wrong time

Come to me, for your home is in my arms.
My arms unlike yours do not act like an alarm,

An alarm that reminds you of me every Wednesday
night,
A night so serene, it made you feel I was right.

The right person, wrong time, might not be the ideal
deal.
A deal made with the devil is like fate sealed.

# 7. Proud by proxy

The night seems so quiet,
It makes my head go wild
With thoughts running around,
From where I will be
To where I am from.

For you know who you got,
Explicit or not.

The weight so excruciating
However, makes them proud.

Are you, though, proud of it all?
Or proud of the fact
That they are proud of you, after all?

# 8. The Fifth Plea

You are not mine to call
Maybe never was to begin with.
Yet I saw myself fall,
Hoping to take the fifth.
I wouldn't dare let you crawl;
On all four that is how I live.

I saw you looking at the stall,
The one that displayed a famous wordsmith.
And just like that, I wanted to write you a letter
On a paper drained with coffee,
Dried in the sun, edges burnt.
My thoughts flowing in cursive,
Thinking if it is all just a ruse.

Then I woke up on the floor,
Not colder than before.
They told me there is a way somewhere here,
In my heart, perhaps, was built a door;
The one that should have been locked for sure.

"*There is a key hidden inside a chest*," they said.
Turned out it was in my head.
It resembled the hands that brought me to life,
Not the first, but the second time.

# 9. Sanctuary of Skin

I see sex as an act, a fact, and a pact;
A desire, a fire; dear God, a body to admire.
An escape, perhaps, that traps you more,
An illusion of intimacy that erodes your core.

A rite of passage or an event well planned,
Maybe in cahoots with the stars and the land.
What was supposed to be an expression of love and life
Is now a sanctuary filled with faux passion and strife.

A refuge, a rhythm, a fevered embrace,
Turned into a habit: empty and displaced.
The blessing I sought, the solace I chased,
Now lingers like perfume, but bitter in taste.

Dopamine that lingers in faulty ways
Is enough for a body to feel whole and brave.
A breathless surrender, a dizzying high,
Lost in his touch, just to be crushed under his eyes.

"*It was the freedom*," said a saint,
 Loud enough to quiet the soul and pray.
 No past, no future, just lips and sins,
 Whispering dreams and binding kins.

# 10. The Trial of Smoke and Silence

With hands as red as blood;
My soul was diligently judged,
Not by one, but too many,
For I tried to tell them plenty
That it was not me who killed,
Standing in a room, smoke-filled.

There sat a jury of living and dead,
All watching the little girl bled,
Not knowing where was she stabbed,
Or was it an ordeal well planned?
Improv was it or maybe a scheme?
Nobody knew it was her one true dream

To see the divine,
While believing it all to be a sign
That she was sent to end a regime
As old as time.
Little did she forget that night
That she didn't have another life to redeem and fight.

And I crossed my legs,
Looking up to find no light,
Crossing my fingers
While closing my eyes.
I looked at the girl smile,
Awaiting the verdict for this trial.

# 11. Lies scripted in Cursive

You bluff; you cry,
To cough up stories and lies.
Some are believable and strive,
Some work just enough to forge a mendacious cry.

They see your words, unable to hear them alright.
The sentences get mixed up to form a lie so white
That the night believes you belong with it, with a sigh,
Making it difficult to separate the earth from the heaven
so up high.

You blame the prejudice and find solace in a decoy.
You hear a voice, and you see a boy.

"*A relief it is,*" he says,
Living among the dead,
Working like a dream,
A book well read.

Yet you ended up
With a thousand words unsaid.

# 12. Unfaithful Hours

Once upon a time there was tale well designed
It talked about those who believed in misfortune and
souls being confined.
"Time is a slut" said the first line.
Followed by words that made no sense or rhymed
In a velvet disguise, She flirts with your hopes,
She tells you sweet lies, then pulls your ropes.

She'll look in your eyes, mesmerizing like a sunrise.
Then let you take the fall for you thought you were all
wise.
She'll offer you riches, then burn down your gold,
She'll whisper you secrets, then leave you out cold.
With one hand ticking, Dear God, will she cradle your
youth,
While the other would be busy shattering your version
of the truth.

She slept with beggars, poets, knights, and priests.
She kissed a king at dusk, then danced with a beast.
For it was you  who were at fault
that you judged and teased
The entity she is , A deceitful queen.
A lover of chaos, cruel and unseen.

# 13. To Bear, To Begin

The hold of responsibility, hidden under the skin,
Was tested for durability and voilà, it was ready to begin.

A war, a strike, a call, a brawl
For the right of the man, for the rise of them all.

The hands that never stopped
Weighed in every time and fought,

Against all storms, against all fires,
To look up and see no men all wired

Perfectly the way she was:
Built to bear without applause.

Enough to breathe,
On fragments of peace.

A dose of strength,
When rest was out of reach.

# 14. The boy he was, a man already

His eyes full of innocence,
His bangs hugging his face,
Seeing through shades.
He found solace in grey.

Oh, and his lips so red,
Full of stories, hidden so well.

Hands like an Austrian map,
A destiny crafted by a woman, perhaps.

However, the name speaks for itself:
A broken heart that ends up healing scars
Not only his own,
But of every passerby
Who didn't have the courage to speak or die.

# 15. Ink-Stained Solitude

I used to pace, not just on the floor,
Spending hours drifting through dream-clad doors.
Living in a universe not quite real,
Was perhaps my only act of rebellion ; my only seal.

A breath, a blink and I'd be gone,
To realms that shimmered just past dawn.
Into a room washed pure in white,
With huge French windows and curtains that write.

They'd watch me dream both day and night,
Build a world, and put up a fight.
I'd wrap myself in soft white sheets,
And feed my soul those lucid feats.

Wearing a white nightgown, I'd watch myself bleed,
Realizing the more I'd feel, the more I'd heal.
Each word ached like a thorn in my head ;
To write, they say, you must stand on the edge.

Alone, you watch the world unfold
Its cruelty, its myths, its silent gold.
So here I sit, with thoughts deciding my role,
One foot in mist, the other in the fiction where my
phantom thoughts uphold.

Walking, walking ; without counting the steps,
A dreamer turned into ink's closest friend.
A poet's gift, a curse, one of a kind:
You lose the crowd... and end up finding your mind.

# 16. The Name I Never Say

I think about the letters that form his name,
Not out of desire, nor out of fear,
But out of sheer desperation and hunger to be clear
To be witnessed, to be seen,
To give meaning to my memory,
To not end up as an accessory to a dream.

Years passed, altering what I remember,
For the brain edits and omits what it cannot explain, and
surrenders.
A dystopian vision that comes to life.
The last time we spoke,
He told the world he was all alone
Little did I know, he had always been.

I was a season he never lived through,
A ghost he used to call Boo-Boo.
Still, my mind won't let it rest,
As if reviving a rumor that the heart is trying to forget,
Rewriting the story that only existed in the hours
Between boredom and sex.

So no, I cannot say his name,
For it is forbidden to speak about
What was never claimed.
Instead, I write a chronicle of a silence,
A monument to a wound
That never bled nor cried.

It taught me how to endure without reason,
To be okay to be read like a book in a prison.
I discovered that love is not always loud,
And closure doesn't come with an ending.
I carry the ache like a half-read poem
Open, unfinished, and still worth keeping.

# 17. He Knows the Weight

No soul is burdened beyond its flame,
Each trial is carved gently, in God's name.
The ache you carry in your chest,
Was known to Him ; a sacred test.


You tremble, yes but do not break,
For every breath, He helps you take.
The mountain placed before your feet,
Was drawn by hands divinely sweet.

He counts the tears you never show,
And waters strength from all your woe.
The silence where you feel alone,
Is where His mercy gently shone.

So bear the storm, though winds may bend,
Each wound will close, each night will end.
He wrote your path, with both fire and rain,
And placed within your soul the desire and pain.

A pain that leads where light still glows,
Carving roads your spirit knows.
The pull of fate will test your mind,
But faith, in time, is what you'll find.

# 18. Between the Lines, I Found Myself

In silence deep, when no one knew,
The world felt cold, the sky not blue.
A shadowed heart, a hollowed soul,
I searched for something to make me whole.

I found escape on glowing screens,
In Wattpad tales and teenage dreams.
Each plot a door, each line a thread,
That pulled me back from thoughts I dread.

From modern myths to Shakespeare's prose,
I found the thorns beneath the rose.
And every book, a lantern's light,
That helped me survive the longest night.

A soul once lost, now confident.
Not every hero wears a name
Some lives in between the lines,
Their voices soft, yet so divine.

# 19. The Man He Became

The voice of the soul,
Once soft, once bright,
Now muffled beneath
The man shaped by fright and fight.

His world now holds
The ties by blood and name,
Forgetting the hands he once held,
And the hearts he once called his *safe*.

The passwords got lost in transition.
Every soul he ever touched was abandoned
At least once, if not twice.
And the echoes of their silence became his only
recognition.

A man who once said
He'd die for the woman who gave him birth
Turned out to be the one
Standing in front of a jury

Accused of uxoricide.

And he who smiled had no remorse of any sort in his
dead eyes,

As if he had known it all from the very beginning of
time,

That love was fleeting and tragedy was the one true
divine.

# 20. Aren't We a Kind of Love?

"*Aren't we a kind of love?*" asked my friend.
Thinking about the weight of his words,
I begin to introspect:
What is love, if not a choice?
If not a rule, but a dice?

"*A good friend,*" they said, "*is a result of your doing.*"
Well, isn't my doing a loving act of my ruins?

The idea is not far from the truth, though
Our Krishna, our Lord, adheres to it and shows
A living example of friend and of life,
For he is the truth and he is the lie.

# 21. Before It Ends

There's something in the air tonight
A softness, a golden kind of light.
The laughter echoes, the sky leans near,
And for the first time, I feel I belong here.

Feeling the moment
Waiting for the impending doom
I smile at the faces in this half light room
For god knows I'm already mourning

The blooming grace
And its vanishing trace.
A month from now, this will be a memory,
A photograph dressed in reverie.

So I hold it close, this fleeting friend,
This almost-now, this near-to-end.
Let me feel it, bold and true,
The joy, the ache, the perfect blue.

www.ingramcontent.com/pod-product-compliance
Lightning Source LLC
Chambersburg PA
CBHW071234140726
47996CB00007B/2601